I0120931

"In the Woods, we return to reason and faith." — *Ralph Waldo Emerson*

"There I feel that nothing can befall me in life, -- no disgrace, no calamity (leaving me my eyes), which nature cannot repair. Standing on the bare ground, -- my head bathed by the blithe air and uplifted into infinite space, -- all mean egotism vanishes. I become a transparent eyeball; I am nothing; I see all; the currents of the Universal Being circulate through me; I am part and parcel of God. The name of the nearest friend sounds then foreign and accidental: to be brothers, to be acquaintances, master or servant, is then a trifle and a disturbance. I am the lover of uncontained and immortal beauty. In the wilderness, I find something more dear and connate than in streets or villages. In the tranquil landscape, and especially in the distant line of the horizon, man beholds somewhat as beautiful as his own nature." – *Ralph Waldo Emerson*

DEDICATED

TO

RICHARD

PATRICIA

AND

NICHOLAS DENUZZO

Introduction

Authenticity

What is authentic? This is the question, among others, that occupied my mind when I decided to enter the forests, prairies, valleys and waterfalls of Charleston Falls Preserve in January of 2013. I went in without any tangible idea of what I was doing or what I would discover. Although I didn't realize it at the time, a specific desire, in fact the reason I endeavored to enter Charleston Falls, did walk through the entrance with me.

Saying I didn't have any preconceived notions is a bit untrue. I had read and admired the writings and philosophy of Ralph Waldo Emerson, Henry David Thoreau, and other transcendentalists. In my opinion they tapped into the same desire, I strongly believe, each person has within them, the desire for the authentic. People have and will continue to call this desire by different names; what is real, enlightenment, truth, peace, genuine, and so on, but what they are all essentially about at their core is authenticity. What drove Thoreau to enter Walden Pond and stay for two years, two months, and two days? He sought the authentic.

It doesn't matter what time period we happen to live or consider in our hypothetical conversations, anyone who has lived in a time period involving human society can relate to the feeling of unconscious imitation permeating into the way we think, act, and feel from society. The feeling of countless human interpretation built up over thousands of years that have been shaping attitudes, ways of thinking, acting, and feeling, and which defines the rules and makeup of society. Seeing people unconsciously conform their behavior to a range of normalcy, that seems and feels like each person has a public persona that can be described as enforced normalcy. In a world we live in today, or the world Thoreau lived in, how can we weed through the seemingly countless layers of years of human interpretation to discover the truth, the uninterpreted truth? How can we disentangle and remove the behaviors and ways of thinking forced on us unconsciously by society? How can we remove all of that to get to a base, where we can then consciously choose what will influence and affect us? In short how can we live an authentic life?

All these questions and the quest for the authentic are what motivated Thoreau to enter Walden Pond. He sought to remove himself from society to enough of a degree to allow independent thought and contemplation. This involved periods with minimal to no contact with other human beings, in order to achieve minimal human interpretation on his thoughts. But what environment could offer that type of seclusion from human interpretations? Any place with human cohabitation would be out of the question. For Thoreau and the transcendentalists they turned to nature. They saw nature as the least interpreted environment available on earth and thus, one which to learn from and discover wisdom. For Thoreau and the American transcendentalists, there was much virgin[1] land around from which to explore, experience, and from which learn. Nature was free of human interpretation of any kind, especially in the relatively recently discovered and sparsely populated North American continent. It merely existed. This was an environment the transcendentalists could study and learn from. Applying the lessons they learned from nature to human society. Not only did nature offer a respite from society, but it was a classroom from which to engage in learning. A place free of human interpretation to study how beings in nature interacted with each other and from which to draw insights. To the traditionally religious, studying nature offered a path closer to God. Undisturbed nature remained as God had created it, how God had intended the world to function. The lessons gleamed from nature would be lessons learned from God, that was free from years of built up human interpretation layered on taking into account countless petty human agendas. The authentic meaning of God What nature offered was the chance at something real, something uninterpretted, something authentic.

The search for the authentic in nature by Thoreau and the transcendentalist really isn't any different than the Beat movement, the 60's counterculture, the modern day hipsters movement, or what each and every one of us in our daily lives, many without realizing, seek in our pursuit of what is cool. At the end of the day, when one deconstructs each movement down to its core,[2] they are all after authenticity. Each movement differed only in what it used and the methods for finding the authentic. The Beats were on a perpetual search for the authentic, constantly traveling across the country and the world after what they sought. Not shying away from any experience or the pain it brought, in order to feel what was real. Fighting corporate intentional human interpretation forced on the population by Madison Avenue. The Beats utilized the same process, trying to remove the layers of human interpretation to arrive at the truth, authentic reality[3]. The 60's counterculture, born out of the placid 50's, sought to change society and the world for the better. Change into what? They wanted to change society into something more humanistic, less contrived, in essence more authentic. More authentic in regards to the relations between people and one another, because surely brother love was authentically human. They sought to tear down all the layers of human interpretation that were making the world so despondent, producing institutional and personal racism, profit driven greed, and desire for power. Regardless of your thoughts on the depth of their analysis or their assumptions, it is undeniable they were going through the process of removing layers of perceived human interpretation to get to a more authentic society and way of living, often with the use of drugs.

---

[1] 'Virgin' in the sense that it had not been traversed by Europeans.

[2] And I strongly suggest most every benevolent movement throughout human history is ultimately about the desire to find the authentic.

[3] Interesting to note that, the Beats put themselves in an untenable position, since they sought to find the authentic in humans and human inhabited areas. Can a human or place habituated by humans in our present time ever be free from layers of human interpretation? It appears they were just running from one human inhabited area to the other, never able to separate the layers of human interpretation and never finding what they were after. The transcendentalists solved this problem by removing humans completely. It seems they were setting themselves up for disaster, not even giving themselves the possibility of finding the authentic, because their methods were philosophically flawed. The whole business seems desperately depressing to me.

Although the Beats and the 60's counterculture were the two most prominent and readily identifiable compatriots of the transcendentalists, each one of us living today who has ever desired something, worn something, purchased something, or gone out with someone motivated by the fact that it or they were 'cool,' is also searching for the authentic. I strongly suspect that what is at the heart of how we define what is 'cool' in our modern vernacular is exclusivity. Each 'cool' item or event has, on vary degrees of depth, an element of exclusivity. It is no coincidence that name brand items, which are often considered more desirable than others, are often more expensive than others. Expensive things in general are exclusive because relatively few can afford to own them. This effect produces many knock off industries; leather, handbags, watches, etc., which leads to certificates of authenticity and the often asked question, 'is this authentic?' The exclusivity of monetary barriers to entry has resulted in the search for the authentic. Even more exclusive than high priced items are items or experiences that have been created specifically for people, also known as original content. A song, poem, a work of art, a joke etc. What could be more exclusive than an original creation that has never been produced or done before? That humans have never experienced before? Also, what could be more authentic that original content? All of which we define as cool. Why do we find creative people attractive? Why are we attracted to people who can make us laugh with original humor? Why are we attracted to musicians, writers, comedians, and actors? They all create original content. Perhaps we are seeking the authenticity in other people. The authenticity sought after by Thoreau and the transcendentalists is pursued by each and every one of us today.

Then of course there are the faux-anti-authentic seekers in the world. The people who seek after and relish what is not cool, what is 'common.' But in a world where everyone is seeking what is cool, what could be more exclusive, and hence cool, then seeking the opposite of what everyone else is seeking, the uncool? In this sense does the search for the uncool have a degree of authenticity about it? Defining what is uncool as the opposite of cool, doesn't achieve a detachment from cool, because what is uncool is still defined in relation to what is cool, what is authentic[4]. Which is still the game we are all playing, what is authentic?

---

[4] As so many faux-anti-authentic seekers do, which consequently is what makes them 'faux'

Seeing the Horizon

However, each movement was and is, in a certain sense, a double edged sword, capable of wandering away from its original intentions, consuming its members. Within each movement are contained the potential seeds of its own downfall. Like almost anything, one can become so consumed with the movement, ideas, or process that the end result is circular and ultimately becomes about the movement. The original goals of those who set out upon their journey become superseded and consumed by the movement's ideas and process. The movement becomes more than a means to achieve a goal or a way of life, it becomes life. And often when adopting this new life, the movement's ideas and process, it becomes a means to escape from the world, from the previous life. The movements devolve into escapism. Instead of shedding light on the world or changing the world for the better, the movements become about escaping the world. Many people of the Beat, 60's counterculture, and modern day hipsters have had their original intentions devolve into escapism. Many lost sight of their original aim and why they even were doing what they were doing. The Beats travelled and reflected constantly, but to what aim? Would you really find the authentic in a new place inhabited by humans? A new City, a new State, a new Country? Sure the next place you went would be a new place with new layers of human interpretations not quite the same as the previous place, but where among any human inhabited place, with all its layers of human interpretation and emanating unconscious imitation, could you find authentic? Could you ever really sift through all the layers of human interpretation to find the authentic needle in the haystack? It seems they were doomed to travel from place to place, never finding what they sought, never with hope of finding what they sought. Doomed from the start. On a perpetual journey which ultimately resulted in escape from human society, place by place. A movement trapped in perpetual futility, which only Sisyphus could relate too.

The 60's counterculture wanted to change the world for the better. To cut through society's racism, consumerism, sexism, and all the other ills and forms of intolerance of society to produce a better place, all of which were built on years of human interpretation that produced current intolerances. A very noble and enviable goal. Using drugs to expand one's mind or alter the way the world is perceived is not strictly detrimental. If used properly can be a very powerful tool from which to employ in analysis. But they also run the danger of allowing one to achieve a type of escape from the world and reality, a perceived separation. While many view the drug counterculture and drugs themselves as the reason the 60's counterculture lost sight of their original aim and become about escaping the world they inhabited, I view drugs only as the means for their devolution into escapism, not the reason why. I don't pretend to diagnose the ills of the 60's counterculture or why they descended into escapism, I'll leave that for those who lived it, myself being born several decades after the fact, but I will offer some thoughts. To my observation it seemed that the 60's counterculture did indeed descend from the heights into escapism. It seems that the movement lacked enough direction and specificity in goals as well as being quite esoteric, to accomplish what they sent out. Perhaps the safety of numbers played a role. The 60's counterculture was a truly massive movement occupying all corners and regions of the United States as well as all socio-economic strata. With so many people how could it fail, how could it be ignored. Perhaps there was a sense that their energy and spirit would carry the day, they were in the right, and the right always win, the truth will always come to light. Without a codified direction or clearly discernable goals, the enormous energy and all its potential was dispersed, unable to bring its full force to bear against all the ills of the world. After a few years, without the world and society changing with the tidal wave of consciousness, perhaps doubt crept in, is our enormous energy not working? Escaping the world became all too easy, and it could be hidden intellectually under the idea of guise of expanding one's mind. With drugs as an outlet, the 60's counterculture devolved into escapism. But escape to where? A world of your own creation, your own mind, an abstraction, any place tangible? Without anywhere to go, the energy was channeled into unproductive means, in regards to changing society. Their idea of creating a more authentic world, in which the evils of human interpretation were brought down, dissipated with their energy.

The Transcendentalists too had the danger of devolving into escapism and many did. Going into the woods in order to achieve an enlightenment or new understanding carries with it the danger of never leaving the woods, or physically as well as mentally escaping from the word and society. When venturing out into the intellectual unknown, mark your path and remember why you sojourned in in the first place, otherwise you can get lost in a woods of your own making.

So I confess, I did have an abstract notion of what I wanted to find, the authentic, but had no idea of specifically what I would find or if I would find anything at all. I flirted with becoming lost on several occasions. I'll let you be the judge of that. It is my first attempt and by no means my last. Hopefully I will improve from what is my infancy with Gonzo-Transcendentalism. What I discovered may very well be common knowledge to you and seem quite pedestrian, but they were very new and important to me at the time.

Gonzo-Transcendentalism

       This is a book about what I learned in the Charleston Falls Preserve. It is a collection of nature journals I wrote throughout the winter, spring, summer, and fall of 2013. The vast majority I have left unedited. At times I have edited certain esoteric passages so that they are perhaps more comprehensible and make sense to those reading them. Each passage is raw and represents most often my stream of consciousness at the particular time I was writing. I want them to be as raw and genuine to my own experience as possible. Hopefully you can experience nature as I did, feel what I felt, and think what I did, as best as humanly possible.

       The stylistic elements described in the paragraph above stem from a desire to make the reader's experience as close an approximation to the transcendental experience one has in nature. So the reader is not just experiencing nature from the author's reflections, but is experiencing nature with the author as they experienced it. *Walden*, Emerson's Essays, and other transcendental works are incredible literary experiences, which move and stimulate the reader. Reading each is reading the refined information distilled after reflection from each author's raw experiences. Thoreau's reflections on his thoughts and experiences during his two years, two months, and two days at Walden Pond are neatly presented in *Walden*. *Walden* is an incredible literary experience, presented in a well thought out, logical style. While nature journaling during my time at Charleston Fall, I would often become distracted by my dog Farley or another person. In order to get back into the mindset I had inhabited before I was interrupted, I would read back what I had written the paragraph or two before. My journals were written for me in a stream of consciousness style, which delved into whatever was interesting to me from moment to moment, second to second. When reading back through, I found I was able to recreate the mindset I previous inhabited, but more than that, I was able to closely approximate what I felt, smelled, and thought when originally writing the journal. It was a different experience from reading a well thought out and edited reflection of someone's experience. I realized I was experiencing transcendentalism in a new way that I had previously had not before, what I was experiencing was more raw, more visceral, more honest, and more relatable[5]. By writing in stream of conscious style that was often non-linear and broken, I was able to get as best an approximation as possible to how I was thinking moment to moment while writing, in essence, to recreate my experience with nature as I felt the sunlight on my skin, heard the rush of water flowing down the creek, and getting inside the mind that thought my thoughts. When reading back through my passages I was often able to tap into emotions in a way I had not experienced before when reading transcendentalist prose. In short, the stream of consciousness, non-linear, raw style gave me a new experience when reading transcendentalist literature.

---

[5] This last part, relatable, seems quite obvious since I was the one writing what I would read. I mean more relatable in the meaning of engaging your senses and the ability to make the reader imagine themselves in the same situation, performing the same tasks, smelling the same smells, feeling the same sunlight, and thinking the same way.

I don't pretend that I am the first and/or only person to come to this realization or experience transcendental literature in this stream of consciousness way. And my journal entries may be very different from traditional or other forms of transcendentalist literature; they are often my relations of observed phenomena in nature to politics or philosophy in society or in general. But in the absence of any knowledge on my part of others doing what I have been doing, I am going to go ahead and name what for me is a new style of transcendentalism. The designation of what to call this raw, unedited, first person, stream of consciousness type of transcendentalism came to me during a nature journal, 'Gonzo-Transcendentalism.' I settled on the 'gonzo' designation because of the perceived similarities between the gonzo style of journalism and the style of transcendentalism I was writing. Created and pioneered by Hunter S. Thompson[6], gonzo-journalism is a style where the author involves themselves so much in the action that they become a main player in the plot and action. With my style of transcendentalism, I was and am the main player and the action, and in a more first person, in the moment way than if reading a traditional transcendentalist work about the author's reflections on their experience. The gonzo style edified by the likes of *Fear and Loathing in Las Vegas* and *Fear and Loathing on the Campaign Trail '72*, is a very exciting style. One of the major difficulties transcendental literature has in connecting with more youthful readers and a wider audience is its perception that it is boring and difficult to read. My hope is that the gonzo-transcendental style I write my journals in is more exciting to the average reader. For all of these reasons, I call the style of transcendentalism I wrote in, Gonzo-Transcendentalism.

---

[6] Brought to fruition and its peak with Hunter S. Thompson's *Fear and Loathing on the Campaign Trail '72*.

Process

     As I entered Charleston Falls, I would try and leave any preconceived notions at the entrance and strip away any lingering thoughts or doubts. I wanted to be as unencumbered as possible, so I could react genuinely to anything I encountered in the forest. I tried to walk through the forest and landscape taking in all the light, colors, smells, and sounds. Relaxing my mind and body. When I felt sufficiently relaxed I would find a place of particular interest and sit or stand in place of comfortable reflection. I would try to observe my surroundings as much as possible from all senses, relax my mind, and allow my mind to think as unencumbered by restrictions as possible. I would then try and write as fast as possible my thoughts in whatever order my stream of consciousness spit out. After I had left the forest, I would read and reflect on my raw thoughts.

     Described above is the rough process I endeavored to undertake each occasion I entered Charleston Falls. I was not always success in completely relaxing my mind and body, and certain journal entries will reflect that fact in varying degrees. I hoped to tap into an inner portion of my mind that lay unutilized in its entirety. A portion of the mind capable of deep, broad, macro-environmental reflection, but that is suppressed naturally by our animal instinct to survive. Contemplation is in many ways a luxury of modernity. In our previous existence as human beings relegated to hunting and gathering, almost every day in its entirety had to be dedicated to survival, to staying alive. Spending periods of time in deep contemplation was time away from essential duties, like procuring food, which very often determined whether one lived or died. Out of necessity for survival, we censored our contemplative minds. In our world where we have surrendered certain amounts of our freedoms for the benefit of community and society, we now can afford to spend periods of time in contemplation without detrimentally affecting our ability to provide food for ourselves, how many of us actually grow or hunt our own food?

     I could have perhaps turned to mescaline, but instead I tried to allow nature to calm my mind and open up my contemplative mind. I need much more practice at it. You can be the judge of my attempts. I hope you enjoy.

Fernando Giannotti

"Build, therefore, your own world. As fast as you conform your life to the pure idea in your mind, that will unfold its great proportions. A correspondent revolution in things will attend the influx of the spirit. So fast will disagreeable appearances, swine, spiders, snakes, pests, madhouses, prisons, enemies, vanish; they are temporary and shall be no more seen. The sordor and filths of nature, the sun shall dry up, and the wind exhale. As when the summer comes from the south; the snow-banks melt, and the face of the earth becomes green before it visits, and the song which enchants it; it shall draw beautiful faces, warm hearts, wise discourse, and heroic acts, around its way, until evil is no more seen. The kingdom of man over nature, which cometh not with observations, - a dominion such as now is beyond his dream of God, - he shall enter without more wonder than the blind man feels who is gradually restored to perfect sight" – Ralph Waldo Emerson, *Nature*

Entries of Note

March 23, 2013 – 45

April 3, 2013 – 57

April 4, 2013 – 69

October 30, 2013 – 99

November 1, 2013 – 107

List of Nature Journal Entries

March 4, 2013 – 25

March 8, 2013 – 31

March 15, 2013 – 41

March 23, 2013 – 45

April 3, 2013 – 57

April 4, 2013 – 69

April 7, 2013 – 81

April 10, 2013 – 89

October 30, 2013 – 99

November 1, 2013 – 107

November 4, 2013 – 113

"We apprehend the absolute. As it were, for the first time, we exist. We become immortal, for we learn that time and space are relations of matters; that with a perception of truth, or a virtuous will, they have no affinity." – Ralph Waldo Emerson, *Nature*

Nature Journal

March 4, 2013

Mind the Prairie Grass

Charleston Falls – Prairie

What an adventure. It's beautiful out here, sitting on the prairie deep in Charleston Falls with my friend Farley. A plane just flew by, crossing the sky, disturbing the prairie as much as a bird call would, indistinguishable really. It was flying remarkably close and low to the ground. I find plans to be quite beautiful. I know it defies conventional thinking, but in the forest a plane flying overhead doesn't bother me. By that I mean it somehow seems to find a place in the prairie and forest, it resonates with the landscape, they are not incongruent or mutually exclusive.   It's probably because I've lived near an airport nearly my entire life. Sitting on my back porch at night watching planes descend and take off silhouetted against the cascading reds, blues, and violets of the setting sun. The portrait is actually quite beautiful, augmented by the jet trials of planes weaving a pattern across the fading sky. Planes going somewhere, not really any different than birds really. I guess what I'm getting at is that the juxtaposition of nature and technology can be beautiful and go together. It's funny how these things from earlier in your life or childhood affect your life. What shapes your world view or the lenses you see the world through.

What had happened in the forest to make it the way it is today? What happened in this exact spot where I sit right now? How the minor details of nature affect us. Who will be here in 1000 years or 100? Sitting here in the tall prairie grass, it's easy to get lost in the moment (part of the reason I love forays into nature) and experience the present as an unconnected experience to any other moment in time. It seems inconsequential whether the blade of grass in front of me is this particular blade or another 5 feet away. I'll visit this prairie tomorrow and a year from now, and my experience will be no less diminished by the new blades of grass growing and the ones currently around me dying. I most likely will not even notice, it will not graze my consciousness. I will still have a similar existential and transcendental experience most time I come back. With these observations in mind, does it matter what we do, in the sense of creating something lasting. What I'm writing now, what anyone has ever written. Future experiences in nature will not alter significantly or meaningfully my experience of the forest and prairie, why would what we are doing change the landscape of human interaction forever. It probably will not, that could be very depressing. Perhaps a temptation toward nihilistic thought might overcome me now, it is tempting, but the prairie seems to suggest otherwise. Perhaps it is not important which blade of grass I see and interact with, and it's not important that I will not interact with that particular one and ones ever again, but that in that moment I interact with that blade of grass, that it exists. If for argument's sake that blade a grass had human like cognitive reasoning abilities, and that blade of grass upon careful contemplation, deciding that what it contributed by its existence wouldn't be permanent, and the blade of grass foolishly succumb to the 'what's the point' line of thinking and decided not to waste time living, I and everyone around it would be denied the pleasure it brings to the forest and prairie. If it is just that particular blade of grass that chooses to do nothing, then it will go relatively unnoticed. But if other blades of grass in mass choose to do nothing a not exist as well, I and others will not find the same enjoyment and peace in the forest and prairie. In the moment I'm in the forest, the blade of grass matters, in that moment. Other living and non-living parts of the forest and prairie need that blade of grass to live and form an ecosystem that functions and works. And there perhaps lies the reason for the blade of grass and by extension any person to keep doing and living life. In the moment, what they do matters to other people. Other people need that person to live, to make a functioning society. That person's actions and thus their existence matters to other people, perhaps not for the 100 years, but in that moment, other people need them. Moment to moment what we do matters and we need others living their lives, much like the forest and prairie need each blade of grass to live. I need each blade of grass to have a transcendental experience in the prairie at Charleston Falls. Another point I gleam from these thoughts are that we have obligations to all other living people. The forest needs each blade of grass. The hawk needs the blades of prairie grass to provide shelter for field mice and so on. We are all interconnected and need each blade of grass to function. We have responsibilities to keep on living and pursuing our pursuits, at the least, to our fellow human beings. Perhaps in this way we can construct vague building blocks towards guidelines of a universal morality. We just have to keep the blades of grass in mind.

Another plane just flew overhead....

I can learn so much from nature. I am trying to choose how I would like to coexist in nature(society) with the greatest respect for others and myself. What are my obligations? The lark chirps, and the other animals allow it. How can each individual sing their song while everyone else allows them to. Not only do we have to live and sing our own song, but we need others to let us as well, otherwise the possibility for destruction exists. Adds another wrinkle. Individually problematic, but in the macro sense, non-consequential. It matters to us, but not to society as a whole. Similar to the field mouse and the hawk. The fish in the pond doesn't care, but it is quite important to the field mouse. Our individual trials and injustices matter to us, but in the grand scheme of things, not to others in our time or the next. Only when they cease to be counted in the realm of the individual and thus counted in large numbers that we arrive at a collective problem which affects all of us in a society. At times we come together with our problems and burn down the prairie.

I feel closer to god in the forest. Among the least interpreted settings of his creation. It's very difficult to disentangle all the centuries of built up human interpretation in our lives.

So much builds on each other. Observing nature and this prairie is a window into an uncorrupted world, or at least substantially less tampered with world. It doesn't have day after day, year after year, century after century of human additions and interpretations. By observing nature and how it acts, we can see a raw, substantially less interpreted view of the world. In a Judeo-Christian setting, a place closer to what God originally created. Stripping away the levels of human interpretation and breaking things down to their core is a useful skill to learn in the prairie and nature.

Nature Journal

March 8, 2013

Plane Lake

Charleston Falls – The Falls

It's been an incredible day at Charleston Falls. Right now I'm at the falls. The snow is melting and the water is roaring over the falls. I don't know what about water really fascinates me and calms me down, but it does. There is something so beautiful about the power of the falls; Water falling and falling, seemingly endlessly, seemingly bounded perpetual energy. (At this moment I watch my shadow against the rock and water of the falls. It seemed important.) I love all the little streams of water that are independent from the main falls coming off, some from inside the rock. There are still icicles clinging to the rock with desperate ease. From the start to the end of the falls, it is a seamless transition of contrast. Snow still exist all around the falls, although it's melting as we speak. The water from the melting snow cascades over the falls, falling together into the rocks below, then out into a tranquil creek, so calm and flat, surrendering no clue of its calamitous fall. It all blends together without pause, and repeats millions of times a minute. The steam coming off the bottom of the falls is quite explicit and fleeting. God I love this place. I don't think I'm quite a nature journaller yet, but in my own time and own fun I will be. I have to do it in my own way. This process I'm endeavoring to undertake is not a process about finding myself, it is a process about creating myself. The reason I'm standing in front of the falls right now is that I want to strip away outside influence as much as practically possible. I'm headed down a path, unencumbered or rocky, each bend shapes me. I seek to see what my own mind can produce. I not only want to remove myself from society's unconscious imitation and interpretations, but to shed away layers of human interpretations that I have grown up with, that have been socialized into the way I think, view the world, and have constructed myself. In absolute terms, it's an exercise in futility, but useful in understanding who I am and in creating who I am.

While nature is the one unifying thing to all who experience it, our interpretation of it is different and unique to each of our minuet perspectives. It has an existential quality to experiencing it, nature, but how we interpret that experience is different. With the sun illuminating this in just the right way it seems close to perfect. Perhaps we shouldn't be afraid of giant violent cataclysmic change, unless you are the rock on the bottom of the falls. Maybe lives need to change with a huge constant surge, but what constitutes that is what we debate aloud. Perhaps the change is necessary to get to where we need to go. How can the creek above the falls circumnavigate the cliff to water the valley below. Almost all the water that goes over the falls makes its way to the creek in the valley. Perhaps the water has an obligation to the forest to take the plunge, without it the valley would not be able to thrive the way it does. So much more I want to say.

The Prairie

      The ballet of planes in the sky. Maybe it is because I grew up near an airport but I love watching the jet trails of planes in the sky, especially when the sun is setting with all the colors at sunset. I'm standing in the prairie at Charleston Falls and looking away from the prairie at the sky, (From up, from downhill because I'm standing in the prairie) as the sun sets, watching the planes weave their jet trails across the setting sun sky. The jet trials absorb all the brilliant blues, reds, and oranges of the setting sun, creating contrast and vivid miniature chiaroscuros. The jets create almost unique clouds. They are also appealing on another level. Each plane is flying up towards the sky, going somewhere. Anyone who wants to experience the world, can relate to that sight. As the sun sets, they are escaping darkness, what I wish I could do each night as I lay in bed. Absolutely beautiful. The juxtaposition of nature and modern, man-made technology is so beautiful. I love it, ever since I was a young boy. It's man made natural art. So exquisite. We shouldn't fear modern technology ruining nature in every instance, because sometimes it can be quite beautiful. Perhaps we are too concerned with disturbing nature and less with a having a relationship with nature. Not a one sided give-take relationship, but one where we each contribute and learn from each other. Nature and technology can coexist. Many mainstream liberals (I'm not a conservative) and the liberalism that's in vogue now should learn this. I will always find this beautiful I suspect, even when I'm over 100.

Nature Journal

March 15, 2013

Attempt

Charleston Falls – Prairie

I'm at the prairie right now. It's beginning to rain a bit. Just teasing with rain at the moment. Watching Farley play in the dead grass. It's overcast and quite dark right now, it feels nice. I wasn't entirely inspired to write but thought I'd give it a go. Now its pouring, until next time.

Nature Journal

March 23, 2013

Transcendentalism and Nature

Charleston Falls – The Creek that Leads into the Falls

Absolutely beautiful. The way the light hits and reflects off the clear, almost nothing of the water is so sanguine, so explicit, it creates a peace and tranquility encompassed in a moment that you could almost live in. A moment that transcends time. It's very peaceful. There is a family that is arguing about crossing the creek on the steeping stones behind me. Kids are for, the parents against. It doesn't phase the creek, they are an annoyance, but not a disturbance, I was still able to experience the creek. It is still so peaceful. I could stare at this creek for hours, from every little detail. The water bug jumps/gliding/skimming across the surface of the water. It's a really cool juxtaposition of the peaceful calm flow of the creek and the flow of the water going over the falls yards downstream, the sound it makes.

Is this creek an escape? Would it be good to actually live here in this moment.(?) Is the time I spend here just a drug, an escape, just another way to get away from my problems or just another way to distract myself from thinking about them? The idea of nature as an escapist element. Am I just coming here and trying to find peace to forget about my conscious; my future, what kind of job should (not want) I get, that girl(gps) I can't seem to get out of my mind.

Do we do that, with nature? If that is true, then is nature any different than the way most people use television or drugs?

I am inclined to say no. At least, the transcendentalist inside me is inclined to say no. While I've been here, I haven't forgotten my problems, they are still here in my mind, ruminating around. I and the transcendental, go to nature for answers to our problems. Or perhaps to clarify, our concerns, or shed new light on them, or perhaps to strip them down to their more basic/nature elements. I seek to find knowledge or truth in the stream. I want to use how the stream functions to view my concerns. Nature is my workshop, I seek to use it to illuminate my text(my concerns).

In all this way, my trip to nature is very spiritual. Nature is very close to how god created the world. By going to god's least contaminated part of earth, we can try and determine how god thinks, without all the human involvement and interpretation.

Also, I do not just come to nature to illuminate my concerns, but also, my joys. We do not talk about nature and our joys much. But they are the ones I enjoy the most. I find my greatest happiness in nature contemplating my joys.

Charleston Falls – Overlook of the Ravine

Incredible scene with the sun in the top right corner of the ravine. A group of guys walked by, I like that they are here, walking by. I feel that I would prefer that to no one, and being in complete isolation.(Thought of gps just now when writing this here). Makes the forest more pure. People were intended by god to be here, they should be here.

The way the light hits through the trees in incredible. It hits one in particular and some to illuminate the entire pine tree. (I should be more descriptive with my thoughts) Wow, just a web of sunlight passing through the trees.

You can't just go away from all your problems, escape into nature, to enjoy peace, to find peace. All you have accomplished is an absence of distraction, really an absence of a lot of things, and in my opinion an absence of peace. Right now I can hear families, parents, children. But what I hear most and what rings true is the laughter of children. It perfectly and seamlessly complements the beautiful web of sunlight through the trees, it perfectly and seamlessly complements nature. Peace is about illumination, coming to an understanding with your concerns, which you can't do in their absence. That's why transcendentalists don't seek peace in nature, they seek to come to an understanding with their concerns, that is how they define peace. And though this illumination or understanding, they can solve their problems/concerns, with the help of nature, the transcendentalist's workshop.

I don't know where I was going with that, but this overlook scene, with the web of sunlight is beautiful. Peaceful (?)

Charleston Falls – Prairie

I'm at the prairie again, I've come to really identify with this spot. The open expanses are beautiful. This will probably be my last entry today.

Shadows are very present here in the setting sun over the open field. I like this, this kind of open, it is like what I have right now in my life. I'm open. I like, although at times I yearn for structure, clear goals, a job. The sunlight warms me. Farley is trying to get at a passing dog while a lark chirps in the background. The prairie is like a golden field.(more traditional field) The moon in coming out.

I have to surrender to my desires to ruminate over my concerns and then very importantly relax. Relaxation and being honest is what is required for transcendental meditation.

I will learn from this prairie

Observation

Pond – The pond is coming alive again. Oh spring.

Nature Journal

April 3, 2013

Gonzo-Transcendentalism

Charleston Falls – The Creek that Leads into the Falls

Spring is finally here. I was looking at the falls from the overlook and they are beautiful. I got the first sense I've had in a long time that spring is finally here. It's that incredible early Ohio spring, kind of warm right now. You still need a jacket, but it feels incredible. I think you need that contrast of winter, bleak and desolate, to really enjoy this type of warmth and spring in general. It's such a fleeting sensation that if you weren't looking for it and appreciating it, it would pass you by.

It's so relaxing. The water so clear, translucent, truthful. It looks like the water isn't disguising itself one bit or there is almost no distortion when looking in. You can look through its essence with ease. It appears the water is being very truthful today in the warm spring sun. Or maybe it's not and it's the best liar of all. Only Farley knows the truth, he's been in and sniffed and seen with his own eyes.

I just had a thought that came to me in a flash. Gonzo-Transcendentalism. I've been reading a lot of Hunter S. Thompson, mostly "Fear and Loathing on the Campaign Trail '72," what if you could combine a Walt Whitman style of free-flowing prose, stream of consciousness, Gonzo style art/literature with the Emerson and Henry David Thoreau Transcendentalism I have loved. I have no idea what it would look, sound, taste, or feel like. (The sound of children playing again, complements nature like the birds from a journal ago ☺) The Gonzo style of journalism has much in common with the human experience of nature as described by Emerson in 'Nature' and Thoreau. Reading a Gonzo account, the narrator or journalist exerts themselves so much into the story and action that they become a central character in the action and story itself. Applying this to writing about transcendentalism could produce some very interesting results to read. Hopefully reading the account of a transcendentalist in nature would produce the feeling, while reading, that one was experiencing nature as the writer was experiencing it. The reader would experience nature as the writer did at the same time. So it would be more of a firsthand account of reflection than reading about a person's thoughts after the experience had occurred. It would be more raw, first person, more natural. During school, many of my classmates were bored by Thoreau and Emerson, perhaps making reading about transcendentalism more exciting could expose the genre to more people, educate more people about transcendental ideas. It would still be transcendentalism, but presented in a different way. Transcendentalism just written in more of a Gonzo style. The world changes, technology, social sensibilities, culture, possibilities, why not update the genre or present transcendentalism in a new light to reflect the changes that have happened in the world. Make it much closer to raw nature journals.

The birds chirp as the sun magnanimously reflects off of the truthful water. Incredible.

Maybe the motto of Gonzo-Transcendentalism is that "the truth, God, is all around-us, it exists today, it's just not evenly distributed." I would write for hours more, but I want to see the falls in this current light and warmth, and my dog Farley is whining to leave. I could sit and write for hours though...

30 feet down the Creek

The water and the bottom of the creek look a lot different here, when compared to earlier up stream. The water seems almost stagnant, truly calm. But an unsettling calm. It's not, but I am suddenly reminded of Walden Pond. This part of the creek no longer looks pristine. The bottom appears to be caked with this dully, intractable mud. Is this like the conventional view of life we take? Does this part of the river combined with earlier part upstream and the (yet unexplored) part downstream represent three general spirits of life?, roughly categorized.

The sun doesn't even seem to reflect beautifully, if at all from this middle part of the creek. Even farther down, much closer to the actual Falls it seems like the previous, first part of the creek, brighter and full of life, just more dangerous (the falls probably). The sun reflects off the water down there, throwing its warmth right back into the face of the observer.

Back to the life thought. Is this dismal middle part of the creek like the middle adult part of life? The one controlled by the seemingly overbearing interests that one seems not to be able to do anything about and just have to conform to. You feel stuck, like the mud at the bottom, trapped in casual ineptitude. The first part of the creek I've just recently written about is like childhood up through university. It's about fun and being yourself, learning and experiencing new things. You are just discovering what your mind and body can do, sex, the world, even dating is a kind of learning and new experience. It's a more reflective time, one where the sun shines beautifully on what you do and the water in front of you. Things are simple and clean/uncovered as the view through the water passing in front of you.

The first part of the creek representing childhood/university years, the second muddled and sullen part representing typical adult/life and responsibility, and the third right before the falls representing old age right before one takes the eternal plunge over the falls.

I am trying to find or decide where the transition point to the middle part begins. Very difficult. Probably depends on what side of the creek you're on. It's probably different for different parts of the creek, its different for each person. Maybe this stagnant muddied bottom part of the creek is the adult/working world. Is this what it means to be an adult?. The light doesn't reflect here, it's monstrous and stagnant. Even more, I'm unenthused. I guess, not much more to say about this, wait I'll try. What does the mud on the bottom mean. Is the beautiful rocks and pebbles covered by the overwhelming cumulative interest of the adult world? Are they preventing this creek from looking beautiful? Are they covering up what the sun needs to illuminate and shine off of? Are corporate interests, which make those willing players of the adult world conform, covering the beautiful potential of this creek? Why has the mud gathered here and not back there(previous part of the creek symbolizing childhood/university)? I don't know. The more I look, the more defined the creek bed is, but it's still covered. The creek appears to be deeper, here. Maybe this part has more serious concerns, having a family, making/earning enough money to eat. With dead parents or without dead parents, the traditional safety net of the childhood/university world, navigating life on your own. There's more room for the muck to sink, with the slower moving water(moving slow because of the depth). It's easier to get bogged down here. It's more complicated. A few water bugs still roam here. Is this the place in life where we are most susceptible to succumbing to all the unconscious imitation that influences the way we think and talk? Mentally muddying and gumming up our minds. Is this unavoidable? How can you not get bogged down? How can you avoid the pressures and circumstance derived by the necessities of the adult/working world. People have probably been asking that same question since the dawn of time. People probably standing in this same spot. I need to write more about this spot but I am going to move on, a bit unhappily I might add.

The water runs fast to the next part(and the last part of the creek, then you go over the falls) The light shines in and reflects off the surface. This part of the creek is like the last part of life. Once you have receded from the adult world. You don't have the cares you use to, a bit more like the childhood/university world, but with louder violent undertones, the falls(death), which you can hear constantly. Quite the contrast. You will soon go over the falls. Still beautiful.

(Note – at this point I had to cut short my journaling. A ranger was fast approaching on a four-wheeler and I didn't want to get another ticket and banned from the park. I bolted just in the nick of time to make to the main trail.)

The Falls

Waiting for my shit blackberry to restart. It keeps restarting for no reason. Watching the whitewater as the falls cascade and crack/crush the rocks below. Beautiful. Is this the scene after you die? (Can hear the sound of children playing in the background)

Nature Journal

April 4, 2013

Common Unifier

Charleston Falls – Valley Overlook

    I can hear a woodpecker. There is a fallen tree to my right(on recollection is was actually to my left), broken into three pieces. It seems I've noticed a lot of things in nature and human life seems to come in threes. It's too early for the web of sunlight between the trees to appear. Still remarkably beautiful though.

    There is a quite still to the forest right now, with the sound of planes in the background. An incredible still, even(my dog) Farley is still, listening with the utmost attention. What can I learn from the forest? Why has it gone silent? Listen and respond. Respond genuinely from impulse. Give the forest back the truth is so generously allowed one to borrow. I do not know.

Creatures are moving, but I can't detect them. Maybe sometimes in the beautiful sunlight we need silence. Maybe it is good to rest. Maybe it is good to examine ourselves. This is not tranquility. Perhaps tranquility is not just a state of physical peace, a peace derived from one's outside circumstances and environment. One cannot just go into the forest, removed from everything and discover tranquility. Tranquility requires a sense of mental understanding as well. The transcendentalist goes into the woods not to achieve a temporary reprieve from society/the world, but to reflect and come to an understanding on their problems from society/the world. Transcendentalism is not about escapism, one doesn't go to the forest to escape from society/the world, one goes to the forest to shed light on the problems and nature of society/the world. One goes to the forest to find a place of sincere contemplation, a place where they can utilize their mind in its best way, in its original way, free to think in an environment where the shackles of enforced normalcy, circumstance, and unconscious imitation from society/the world have been removed. In a way it is like practice for living in society/the world. A basketball player goes to an empty court and works on their jump shot without all the distractions, the cheering/booing fans, pressures, teammates, and a defender or two in their face. They perfect their shot in the gym in a way that would be all but impossible in an actual game like situation. The transcendentalist does this in nature, free to think in an original way that would be incredible difficult within all the pressure of society/the world.

I don't know why. I want to know why this is happening.

(Note – at this point Farley jumped up on my notes and left a muddy paw print on the lower portion of the page. He's not finding it tranquil either. As usual, Farley is a better judge of a person or place's character than I am, so it's probably time to push off)

It feels almost like a vacuum, a pine tree blows in the breeze, ever so slightly. It looks like the sunlight is gently moving in's branches. Perhaps I have disturbed the forest. Is this the forest's way of telling me, I should not be here? Perhaps it is time to move on.

Charleston Falls – The Falls

Looking out onto the Falls from the lower observation deck. Got some great pictures of the falls off the trail. Met a fellow companion, who wandered off the path and behind the falls. Small moments of comradely. I think Farley really liked the Falls as much as he can while being scared of them. I want to cherish this time it the falls, because when spring is over, the water will stop following and summer will be upon us.

I love all the nooks and crannies, different levels, and meandering path ways the water takes when it hits the rocks from below. Infinitely incredible. The water falls from such a high distance to reach the rocks below. Every drop of water is taking a leap of faith when it goes over the falls. Every single one. As if they have a choice. Perhaps we are like the them. I'm led to believe that people in general are very risk averse. People like the predictable, the safe. What is less predictable is them taking a leap of faith, but yet the falls seem to tell us that we all take leaps of faith. If we don't, then we end up mulling in the froth at the end of the stream. Maybe we all do it, take a leap of faith in many small ways, like the thousands of drops flowing/cascading over the falls, and that in aggregate all these little leaps of faith add up to one big roaring waterfall. We just can't see them, because they are too small individually. If one thinks about it, every single human interaction requires multiple leaps of faith. Or each interaction is a leap of faith. We just need to stand back and get a better vantage point to see it.

(just saw a guy overlooking the falls. So many people come here, why? What are they thinking about? What problems are they mulling over? Empathy. Do we find self-empathy from)

There are multiple paths and multiple end points for the water that leaps over the falls. Some landing spots may be a bit more forgiving than others, but there doesn't look like much difference to me. I guess it depends on the angle of the rock you want to hit. No matter where you start in life we all end up at the same place. The water keeps flowing, is the Forest or God telling me there is life after death? That it's just part of the stream.

The water even finds ways of coming directly through the rocks, skipping the falls. But it is very little water that follows that path. Perhaps those are the original people, people who are not bound by circumstance and have thrown off the layers of unconscious imitation to enough of a degree. It is an arduous and at times dark bath to avoid the waterfall, but they find it, not many, only the determined, but they find it. Seeking the authentic the original often requires taking a darker path.

Moss is growing on the rocks at the immediate bottom of the falls, even in extreme, violent conditions there is life. For the slow and steady there is life in the wake of extreme, violent action. Perhaps then we must be like the moss and find life to continue to live surrounded by violence. We must keep living and by living provide color to the dark violent parts of the world, like the green moss. The green moss stands out as a beacon, clearly visible, when viewed through the Falls, the cascading water, which impacts the awaiting rocks so violently. The others endure as well. There is moss on the side of this giant dead tree that will soon fall, the moss is on the opposite side of the side the tree will fall on. It seems to be willing it on, willing it to keep standing. As if it is pulling it back. That moss on the tree is a beacon of hope, it has latched itself onto a lost cause, the dying tree, but is setting an example and humanizing the tree. It reminds me of the Tibetan cause and their fight for a free Tibet. It's all but hopeless, but they must keep fighting on, as an example to others. What has that moss inspired? What set of actions has it set in place by its stand?

(Sound of Children laughing on a nearby trail)

I've seen lots of different people coming here to Charleston Falls in all capacities. Couples (young and old), solitary people, families (including the white trash one behind me with four kids, which is ok, except both parents are smoking. Which is why I will be leaving soon and to let Farley run more, it's only fair to him) coming to Charleston Falls. Why do they all come? We all have problems. I think that people are all in their own ways transcendentalists. Maybe not in an everyday Thoreau kind of way, but in their own individual ways. This predates the

Thoreau transcendentalists by thousands of years, but it mean that Thoreau and the transcendentalists were just doing something ordinary, something every person does or thinks about. Perhaps then transcendentalism is a common unifier, a common starting point for cosmopolitan discussions, which can break down barriers and enlighten the world.

On that note, I really can't keep Farley waiting and longer.

Nature Journal

April 7, 2013

Intro to Spring

Charleston Falls – The area across the creek that leads to the long trail

I'm trying to enjoy this time of year, the early to mid-spring. Right now, I'm leaning up against a tree sitting in the dirt, probably with ants running towards my clothing. Farley somehow sitting faithfully by my leg. He's being a good sport.

The area I'm in right now is full of woods, trees, many many trees. It isn't deep enough into spring yet to provide even the inkling that anything is starting to come back to life.

(Can hear the sound of children playing in the distance)

I do love Ohio and the Midwest, the weather patterns at least. In the winter everything hibernates, migrates, or dies. It's bleak. (I'm going to stand up now. I feel things crawling on my back) It's not like down South where everything migrates too, as a destination. In Spring it's like the whole land, ecosystem come back alive. It's incredible. Like watching the rebirth of something bigger than yourself, something that will always be there, something that got along fine long before you were around and something that will get along fine long after you're gone. There's serenity present contentment with that.

This may be one of the last times I'll be able to look right through all of the trees to the ravine beyond. Piercing the foliage right through with its depth derived from death and inactivity. I can see all of the area in all of its spender. I can see the dead log from a large fallen tree, turning red with decay and life, from the horde of terminates swamping and recycling it. All the interweaving of branches of trees overlaid with each other. During the summer and fall, all of this will be covered in green.

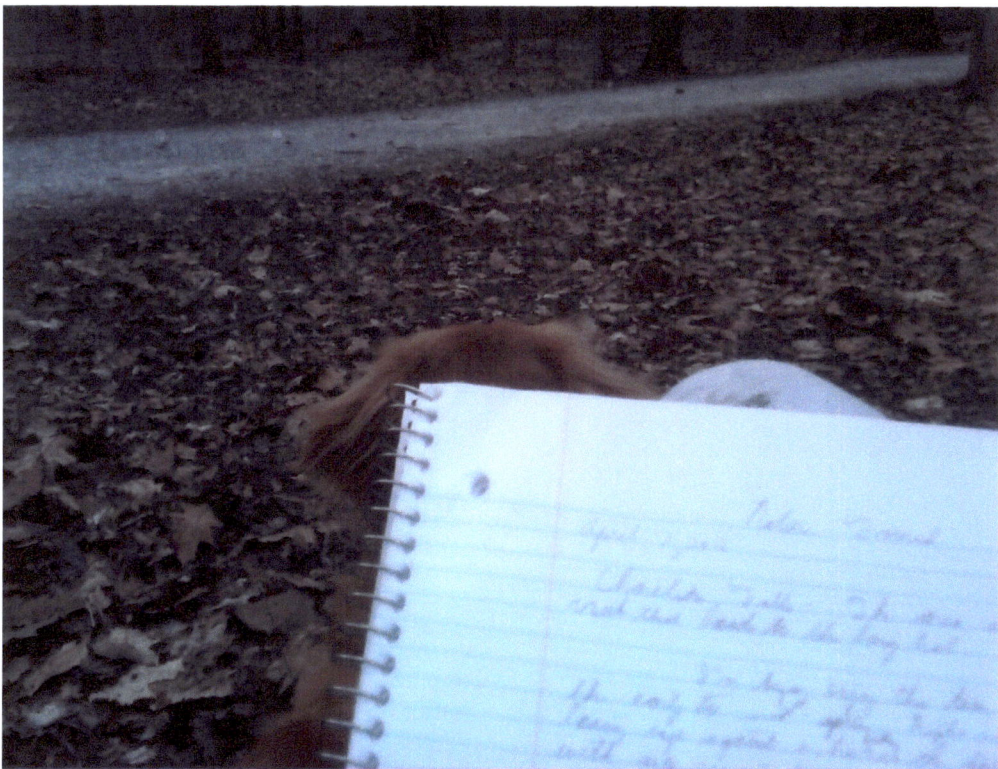

Charleston Falls – The Pond

Spring is back. The smells. The pine trees are starting to smell again. While I was walking along a trail toward the pond (Well before you get to the wooden lookout towers) It was the first time in months I could smell spring.

Multiple birds chirp, while I write. Maybe mosquitoes too, spring really is here. (Hope I don't get west nile) (Can hear sound of children playing)

The water is beautiful to look at, especially with the sun reflecting off of it. The new green hasn't grown back in yet. Everything seems golden; the cattail stalks, the leaves decaying, the sunlight reflecting off all of it and the water.

Nature Journal

April 10, 2013

Ducks on the Pond

Charleston Falls – The Creek which flows into the Falls

I can't take it. It feels like I want to bug out and leave. The isolation is getting to me. Cabin Fever is setting in. I feel like I want to take a job just to take it and get out. I don't think I want away from things as they are, I just need a change. Like I have diminishing marginal returns for concentration. I don't think it's this particular setting, just need a change. It's making me tense. Need to move on.

I have that feeling like I would welcome a bad thing, a bit of pain. It's that feeling of change or boredom that is causing that want. Like I sit on the banks of this creek while my dog plays in the water, but I'm looking up at those clouds above me, those ominous grey clouds and want it to downpour. Probably just because I must have a change, I have that itch. Kind of like when you are driving and have a sudden urge to turn your car into on-coming traffic It's not an urge anywhere strong enough for you to act on, at all, but it's there beneath the surface regardless. More of a feeling than an urge.

I don't know what any of that had to do with nature, I just sat down and had to write it. I may be coming to an end with Charleston Falls. It might be time for a change, as well. It's time to move on, for the sake of moving on, just have that itch.

Charleston Falls – The Pond

    I lied, kind of. It feels like change is about ready to burst, burst from the clouds, burst from the wild ravaging wind blowing ripples across the pond. The birds are all a flutter chirping fast and beautifully. The water on the pond is swirling.

The wind is that delicious, mischievous wind that implies danger is not far behind. It's palpable, thoughtfully delicious. It's as if my hidden desire for change is upon us.

The pond is starting to come alive as well. Today is the first day I've spotted fish. Many of them, Farley scared three birds out of the cattails mere minutes ago. The birds have returned and are busy making up for lost time.

How should I interpret this? (How should I interpret this message from the forest/God?) Is this a call, a demonstration of patience? That if I am too quick to change, I will miss out on the very thing I sought? That I shouldn't give up or dismiss people? If you wait long enough, people will surprise you. Charleston Falls itself, the animals, and the pond have brought about the change, the change came from within. We're all capable of change, we might just need a little wind/outside stimulus. Don't fear the help from others that comes in on the wind. Analyze it, sometime you need it, however small it may seem. Other times it is just wind, and should be ignored.

Why is it, that right before the storm, on the precipice I am most excited? That things are most exciting. I can hear a bull frog. Maybe it is the excitement of the trial to come, with the safety of the before. Excitement with serenity. Liking the idea of something, without actually liking it in practice. It's a precarious in between phase. You have much of the excitement of the event without the danger that comes during the event. It is the best of both worlds, feelings without the responsibility. That desperate time when hope is throbbing through your veins because much is still possible, although dwindling. Perhaps that is why we like that time, the uncertainty is exciting, we can't prepare for the outcome, so it's exciting because of the possibilities. Our imagination takes over in the gab of uncertainty. Once we know what will happen, once the possibilities are narrowed, we lose the space for imagination, which is less exciting. Is the fantasy better than the reality?

What's below the surface? What secrets lay hidden? What's below the surface of my mind? Society? That's really the question. Look at the ducks on the pond. They seem stolid, calm, at ease, but underneath the surface of the water, their feet are probably paddling a mile a minute. Are we all ducks on a pond? Perhaps we should embrace that chaos and worry we seem to all have. Be honest with ourselves, perhaps then we will not have to spend energy concealing it, and make better use of our energy. Or do we need that duality? Do we need space to thrash about without notice? Controlled wanton abandonment in a way. An outlet of energy that doesn't require behavior that pushes other away. An outlet that allows energy to be dissipated while existing in the mainstream. A way to stay sane?

The pond is lovely dark and deep. How may secrets does she keep? (Why she?) Who's looking into the pond? Can anything be in and of itself?

Farley sees a duck treading on the pond.

(Note – At this point I was forced to stop abruptly. I had to chase Farley into the woods and then I got my wish, the clouds opened up and it started raining)

Nature Journal – October 30, 2013

Charleston Falls

Heaven, Time, and Boredom

Charleston Falls – The Creek that Leads into the Falls

It's very relaxing to be back. Fall is not usually my favorite time of year, but I'm very relaxed at the moment. As I'm surrounded by recently shed leaves on the ground and leaves gently breaking their bond with the trees, floating down to earth, and leaves about ready to drop off trees, it feels as though my trips into Charleston Falls are peeling away layers from me, simplifying myself, like I'm returning to my natural state. Like the layers of unconscious imitation are falling off and peeling away. (A leaf just floated down on my leg) I feel freed and unencumbered, independent of the pressures of society which can be trying. This is my outlet for the 'cultural frustrations' I'm backed into by society for my agreement of community power substituted for the individual power. I hear the meager sound of the falls playing in the background with a plane (the sound of) flying over my head. The few remaining birds chirping. Even the water of the creek is so calm and plaid, even though in a few yards it will plunge down. It is calm even with its 'imperfections,' because those 'imperfections,' like terminating over a waterfall are not imperfections they are precisely what makes this creek what it is. Those imperfections are the heart and soul of the creek and of nature. Without those imperfections, without them as a comparison, it would not know beauty…

This place is my sanctuary, it is heaven on earth, but then again the lives we live on earth are heaven on earth. (Another leaf fell on me.) If I died and went to heaven I would hope God would say, before I walked through, the pearly gates, "It's exactly the same." Although I do not think he will say such a phrase. I think he will probably say, "Now you get to look down with envy." (of course this is all presupposing a rather medieval view of God, which I will address later.) Because I think God envies us. He envies us for the same reason many people fear and wish to be like God, he envies us for our mortality. We are doomed, we have a contrast thrust upon us in a sea of seeming randomness. We are all mortal and we will all die. Our next breath could be our last. This makes everything more beautiful to us. We have appreciation. Everything is more beautiful to us because we are doomed. Would chocolate taste as good as it does if you knew you could have it every day for the rest of eternity? We need our death to appreciate our lives. Without it, what would bring joy? I will never be here again. In this moment and on earth, I will never be here again. Everything is more beautiful to us because we are doomed. We will never be here again. Under this guise, heaven seems the upmost heights of miserable. But here and now, it is beautiful. So relaxing, so revealing. Farley is pressuring me to go. Must be off.

Leave the discussions of updating our view of God to another time.

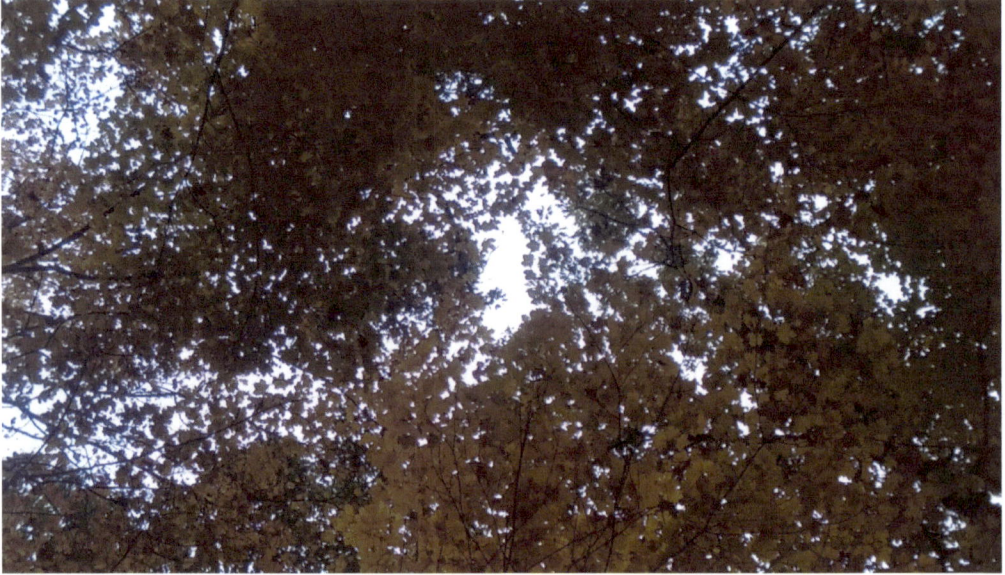

The Ravine

      I'm at the ravine. Its fall and the world is darker, much less sunlight piercing, barely any at all right now. The spider webs of sunlight radiate through the trees and leaves are gone.

Their imprint is still here though. Not visible but connecting every branch, each leaf, and twig together, like an invisible blanket. Many of the leaves are missing from the trees, but most are lost, look no further than your feet to find them. One bird in particular is having a very loud conversation with a few other birds into the night. It sounds all too familiar. This overlooks into the ravine has changed several times I've been here, but it is the same. Time changes but we view it differently, through different lighting and characteristics. Our perceptions change, but we are still looking at the same thing, the ravine.

Perhaps our views of religion, in mass society, need to reflect our new views of religion. In terms of the three Abrahamic faiths, it seems we are stuck viewing them through a medieval frame of reference. We judge them by medieval standards we don't update the way we see and understand religion with the passage of time. We view religion as a stationary static thing not as an ever changing evolving, dynamic force. As our understanding of science has changed, so has our understanding of the world, but we do not apply our new scientific understanding of the world to religion, we do not update our understanding of religion with more information. Using modern science like string theory, particle physics, and evolution, we can help explain God, and shed more light on how a divinity concept could flourish. Determinism based on particle physics could shed light on fate and 'God's Plan.' Science and religion are not incompatible, they just need to be looked upon with the same mindset. I'm also not talking about the trappings of religion, or physical religion practices, but of the idea of religion in general, and speaking of the philosophical tenants of religion. Just because religion was or probably has evolved to explain what humanity couldn't explain, doesn't mean it doesn't still have merit today, beyond an explanation of the unexplained.

Like heaven was probably a way to compensate people for all the hardships and injustices of their time, back in a more violent (by frequency) time. It makes things seem fair and helped people get through, most likely, very tough lives. Today this makes less sense. Given modern health and governance, one is confronted with far less immediate life ending threats. And as I stated earlier, heaven with infinite life would be miserable place, because we do not have the contrast of an unjust and cruel life to make us appreciate a safe life. But use science and perhaps things look a bit more rational. I believe the biggest shackles on our lives is time. Perhaps if time became a malleable dimension, heaven would have a more meaning. Similar to the two dimensional being who cannot image depth, the idea of existing in time would be equally as impossible to imagine. Why don't we use science to update religion.

It is getting darker in the ravine. Shadows are playing their tricks, but it is still the ravine.

Many 'devoted' practitioners of religion make it easy to point and down play religion, but they speak for and represent the trappings of religion, not the religion as an idea. We should stop focusing on the trappings of religion, judging religion by its trappings and start using science in conjunction with religion, updating religion.

With the birds and the smell of pines still so relaxing. And my hand hurts.

Nature Journal

November 1, 2013

Reflections on Thoreau

Charleston Falls, the Pond

       I come to Charleston falls in many ways to escape the pressures of society and unconscious imitation, in society but also in a particular person who embodies and lives all the trappings of an unexamined life. I'm not trying to find myself in nature, I'm out here trying to create myself. Not escaping for the sake of escaping, but escaping deliberately. Escaping so I can think, so I can create myself with the overwhelming powers of unconscious imitation from society and people at a diminished level. So that my own thoughts and discovers are the dominant force shaping me, not the will and power of community, majority government. Like working on your jump shot alone in a gym, perfecting it so it stands out and is effective surrounded by people and the crowd during a game. I identify with Thoreau's disdain of community government and its smothering effects on the individual. In many ways one of the foundations of democracy is the replacement of individual power with he power of the community. Together with the community, we can set up restrictions on individual behavior that allow us to better satisfy basic human wants. Law and order, better protection from injustice. Pooled resources for better food and sanitation protection. We lose many individual powers over ourselves though. While beneficial, restricting human individual power goes against our nature instincts. It is not just governments and constitutions, the physical packs themselves, but our societies that perform the same functions for social norms. This is also a loss of individual power. If this power isn't compensated in an appropriate way or an avenue provided for the frustration, these restrictions on the individual result in cultural/individual revolts or what mainstream society would call cultural perversions. The individual yearning to be free, the through off the shackles of community power. Community power is difficult to attach, it doesn't have a readily identifiable focal point. It is too large and vague. It almost or perhaps is an existential threat. We can't escape it in absolute terms, but we can earn brief reprieves. I feel lighter and unencumbered out here next to the pond. Larks and cardinals are chirping ever so lightly. The sun is graciously washing over my face as it races across the surface of the pond. Farley is racing around the brush and cattails. The sun irradiated the trees, with the deep fall yellows, oranges, ambers, reds, greens, the elusive purple, and pine needles mixed in. Thinking out loud seems organic, seems my own. The pond gives me ownership over my thoughts and myself. It lets me watch, listen, and genuinely respond. It doesn't push itself on me, let's me exist, near it. It seems like it responds organically, not with socially acceptable cliches. The wind blows, ripples swell, the cattails dance, the birds chirp, I prefer that response to any other. If the pond is acting, its doing a superbly wonderful job. In many ways Thoreau was incredibly esoteric, I probably am as well. Perhaps I think I'm relating to him, or I'm making it all up.

The pond, the air, the Sun, it feels just like spring. Even though everything around me is dying, it feels like rebirth is in the air. This maybe the first time I have truly appreciated fall.

I must admit, in all honesty, I came here to escape someone, the person who personifies and embodies all the unexamined, group-think, individuality killing, dis-genuine, fake qualities that derive from the replacement of individual power by community power. There are many like this individual, but I still find the group-think interactions with them insufferable. What is the cost of community power. No doubt we are materially better, but what have we lost? Perhaps this is why each constitution or social pact needs a bill rights or rights of man. We have to place a limit on community power at some point. Otherwise we might be swallowed whole. Perhaps those 'cultural perversions' or natural individual desires are what drives modern fear of government encroachment and makes many of us fight so dearly for those real or perceived individual freedoms. What would Thoreau think? The sun is behind the clouds. If only it would come out one more time.

Nature Journal

November 4, 2013

Being Tall

Charleston Falls - The Falls

I'm in luck right now. The falls still have water flowing down. The sun is breaking through the clouds and branches, slowly warming the world back to life. The sunlight is starting to shine through the falls making it look like cascading crystals. Even the water hitting the black stones at the bottom of the falls are beautiful. With the sun coming out it feels like spring, like the falls have had a new life inserted into them. It looks like the edge of a lake beach sometimes. What I love about the falls is that nothing seems the same. No two rocks or leaves or pebbles or trees, or branches seem to be the same.

The Lookout over the Ravine

The sunlight is back and it is again spinning beautiful webs over the ravine. Elegant barely visible silk like webs across the branches, needles, and trees. Slight breeze and the chirp of a lark. The abundance of pine trees give the illusion that winter is not coming. Wiley trying to trick the observer that spring is around the corner, not its older colder brother. Seems very meditative here. The sun shining onto your face. I get the same feeling each time I come here, the same joy, the same relaxation. Doesn't matter the season, the weather it is the same. Different conditions give the same feeling. Is it fair? Its certainly not equal. Each time I come things are different. I can't recreate that moment in nature, perhaps in my head, but I can't recreate it or remedy it. Can we really be equal as people, if nature in all its splendor can't recreate scenes, what hope do humans have? Often we say we want an equal society, but is that really obtainable. Each person is born with different physical characteristics and different mental capacities, how can we remedy that? Our desires born out of our different circumstances and advantages would just be pushed into something else, that we can't remedy. In this way economic egalitarian principles, in there most extreme form communism, are untenable. Our use of capital as a way to make ourselves better than our peers would be channeled into other pursuits, who is stronger, more physically attractive, etc. Perhaps this is behind the female obsession with beauty, in a world in which women were not allowed to compete economically or otherwise their desires and ways of creating a superior position were put towards physical appearance and beauty. It always finds an outlet. Animals in the forest are all born into different circumstances among species, so are we as humans. Perhaps capitalism is natural, like the forest. Perhaps we should put more emphasis on what we can control, not equality because we are inherently unequal, but in terms of fairness. Should the predatory bird apologize for being a predator? Should a person born tall apologize for the way they are born? Should people who have worked hard to create themselves apologize for their effort?

Fernando Giannotti is a writer and economist from Dayton, Ohio. He is a member of the comedy troupe '5 Barely Employable Guys.' He holds a B.A. in economics and history and an M.S. in finance from Vanderbilt University. A self-labeled doctor of cryptozoology, he continues to live the gonzo-transcendentalist lifestyle and strives to live an examined life.

www.ingramcontent.com/pod-product-compliance
Lightning Source LLC
Chambersburg PA
CBHW040130270326
41928CB00001B/14